The Revolutionary War

VOLUME 5

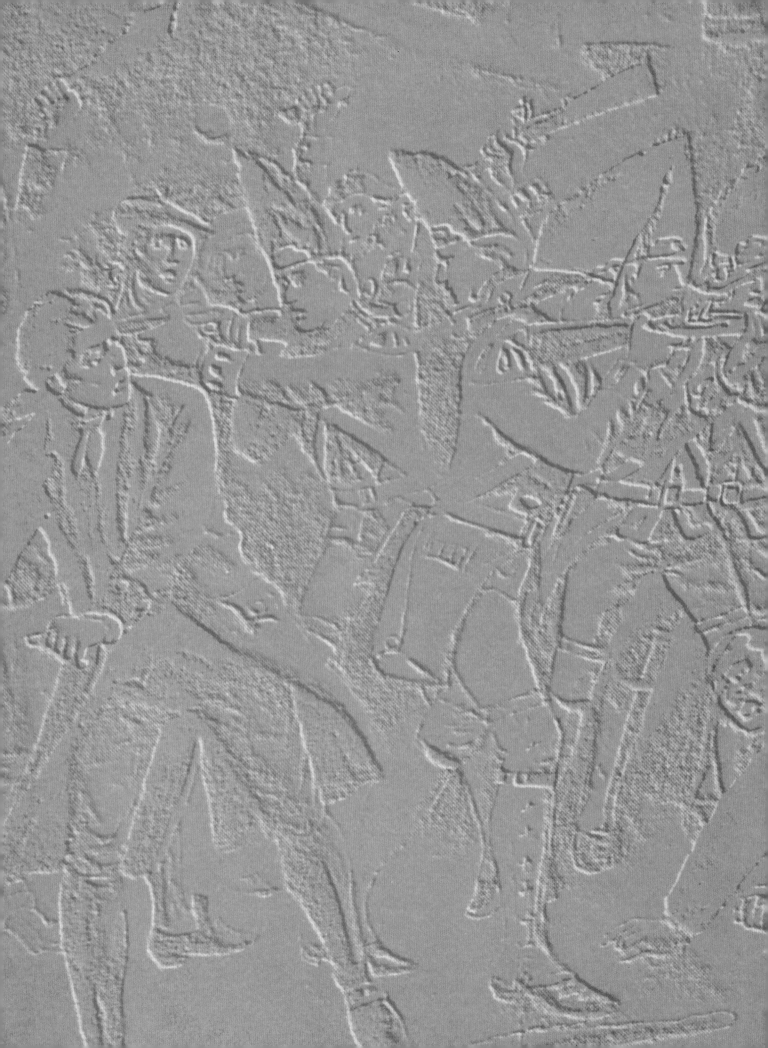

The Revolutionary War

VOLUME 5

1777: A Year of Decision

James R. Arnold & Roberta Wiener

GROLIER EDUCATIONAL

**First American edition published in 2002
by Grolier Educational**

© 2002 by Graham Beehag Books

Grolier Educational,
90 Sherman Turnpike,
Danbury, Connecticut 06816

Website address: http://publishing.grolier.com

Library of Congress Cataloging-in-Publication Data

The Revolutionary War.
    p. cm.
  Contents: v. 1. The road to rebellion—v. 2. The shot heard around the world—v. 3. Taking up arms—v. 4. The spirit of 1776—v. 5. 1777: a year of decision—v. 6. the road to Valley Forge—v. 7. War of attrition—v. 8. The American cause in peril—v. 9. The turn of the tide —v. 10. An independent nation.
    Includes bibliographical references and indexes.
    ISBN 0-7172-5553-0 (set)—ISBN 0-7172-5554-9 (v. 1)—
ISBN 0-7172-5555-7 (v. 2)—ISBN 0-7172-5556-5 (v. 3)—
ISBN 0-7172-5557-3 (v. 4)—ISBN 0-7172-5558-1 (v. 5)—
ISBN 0-7172-5559-X (v. 6)—ISBN 0-7172-5560-3 (v. 7)—
ISBN 0-7172-5561-1 (v. 8)—ISBN 0-7172-5562-X (v. 9)—
ISBN 0-7172-5563-8 (v. 10)
    1. United States—History—Revolution, 1775–1783—Juvenile literature. [1. united States—History—Revolution. 1775–1783.] I. Grolier Incorporated.

E208 .R.47 2002
973.3—dc21   2001018998

Printed and bound in Singapore

CONTENTS

CHAPTER ONE

The Strategy of the 1777 Campaign

The failure of the military to crush the American rebels by the end of 1776 discouraged British Prime Minister Frederick North (left). British Secretary of State Lord George Germain (right) believed that the reinforcements sent to America would defeat the rebels in 1777.

Decisions in London

The winter of 1776–77 found the American and British armies in camps called winter quarters. George Washington's army was in winter quarters at Morristown, New Jersey. The main British army, commanded by General William Howe, was in winter quarters in New York City. During the Revolutionary War large armies in the middle and northern colonies did not campaign (march and fight battles) during the winter. It was too hard for armies to find food and shelter and to move through snow and mud during the winter. So, the large armies rested and got ready for a new campaign that would begin when the weather got warmer. While the armies rested, the leaders made plans, or strategy, for 1777.

On the British side there were two groups of leaders who thought about strategy. One group was the army generals in North America. The other group was the government leaders in London. The head of the British government was Prime Minister Frederick North. The political leader in charge of the war was Secretary of State Lord George Germain. North had hoped that the war would end in 1776. The fact that it was still going on discouraged him. But North knew that the British king, George III, wanted a complete victory against the American rebels. North was deeply loyal to his king. So, North continued to work to win the war.

The campaign of 1776 did not discourage Lord Germain. During 1776 Germain had organized large armies and sent them across the 3,000-mile-wide Atlantic Ocean to America. Those armies had driven the rebels from Canada. They had captured New York, the most important rebel city. They had also captured Newport, Rhode Island, so that the ships of the Royal Navy had a safe harbor during the winter storms.

Germain was disappointed that Washington's rebels had won some battles at Trenton (December 26, 1776) and Princeton, New Jersey (January 3, 1777). (For a description of these battles see Volume 4.) But Trenton and Princeton had been small battles where only a small proportion of the total British forces had taken part in the fighting. Germain did not think that those battles had been very important. He wrote to General Howe to say that the rebels had attacked Trenton and Princeton because they were desperate. The battles were "symptoms [signs] of weakness, not marks of strength."

Germain knew that whenever a large British force had met the rebels, the British had won. For the 1777 campaign the British had three large forces. They were in New York City, Newport, and in Canada. Germain believed that wherever those forces went, they would defeat the Americans. The big question was where to send those forces.

British strategists had always thought that the Hudson River Valley was the key to victory. Their idea was to have the army in Canada march south to the Hudson River. Meanwhile, the army in New York would sail up the river. The two armies would meet somewhere on the river. By controlling the Hudson River, the British would separate New England, the birthplace of the revolution, from the rest of the colonies. That idea was the basis for British strategy for 1777.

The royal governor of Canada, General Guy Carleton, commanded the British forces in Canada. Secretary of

King George III was certain that his duty was to bring the rebellious colonies back into the British Empire.

Above: Lord Germain chose General John Burgoyne to lead the major British offensive against the rebels in 1777.

Below: The Hudson River at West Point

State Germain did not think that Carleton was the right man for the job of leading the British march south into American territory. During the 1776 campaign Carleton had been slow and cautious. The 1777 campaign needed a bold leader. Germain and the Cabinet (the high officials working in the government) chose General John Burgoyne to command the British invasion.

Burgoyne had had an unusual career. When Burgoyne was a young officer, he went to Europe with the daughter of the Earl of Derby. Burgoyne was so poor that he had sold his position, or commission, in the army (in the British army officers bought and sold the right to serve at different ranks). Seven years later the Earl of Derby forgave Burgoyne for going off with his daughter.

Burgoyne returned to the army at the age of 34. As a captain, he served in two raids against French ports. Then, because of his family connection, he received a large gift. He was given the right to raise and command a cavalry regiment. Burgoyne led his regiment in two battles against the Spanish. He proved himself brave and daring. Burgoyne had been in Boston during the Battle of Bunker Hill. Then he went to Canada, where he joined Carleton. After seeing Carleton drive the rebels out of Canada, Burgoyne returned to London.

Service in two raids and in two battles had not given Burgoyne very much experience in war. He had none at all as a general commanding an army. But Burgoyne spoke well, he had important friends, and he knew how to use his friends so he could get ahead. He said that he had a plan to defeat the American rebels. For those reasons the British government named Burgoyne to command the army in Canada. That was to prove a huge mistake.

Burgoyne liked to gamble. Often he lost big sums of money. Because he had married into a rich family, he had enough money to keep gambling. Before he left London to sail to Canada, Burgoyne went to a famous gambling club. There he made a public bet with a friend: "John Burgoyne wagers [bets] Charles Fox one pony [fifty guineas, a large sum] that he will be home victorious from America by Christmas Day, 1777."

Howe's Plans

While Burgoyne was in London, General William Howe was in New York City. Howe was in charge of all of the British army forces in America. It was hard for him to communicate with the government in London so that he

General William Howe commanded all the British army forces in North America.

and the government could work together to make intelligent plans. For example, Howe sent a report on December 20, 1776. It did not reach London until February 23, 1777. Even if the government quickly replied to Howe, at least another two months would go by until Howe got an answer from London. During the four months it took to trade ideas, many things could change to make the ideas useless.

For example, by December 20, 1776, one of Howe's generals, Lord Charles Cornwallis, had conquered most of New Jersey. At that time thousands of New Jersey loyalists (people loyal to the king, also called Tories) were helping the British. About 2,500 New Jersey loyalists had enlisted in the British army. Howe's letter of December 20 described his strategy for 1777, and it was based on all of this good news.

But even before Howe's letter was halfway across the Atlantic on its way to London, dramatic changes had taken place. George Washington had led two surprise attacks at Trenton and Princeton. Because of the rebel attacks the British had abandoned most of New Jersey. The New Jersey loyalists who had been helping the British then left the British army to defend their homes against the rebels.

The British leaders needed a solid strategy to follow even when things changed. The plan for Burgoyne to march south from Canada while Howe marched north from New York was one example of that kind of strategy. If the British followed the strategy, the two biggest British armies would work together. But, because of Trenton and Princeton, Howe decided that he had to make a new strategy.

Howe decided to capture the rebel capital at Philadelphia. He would take most of the army in New York and lead it against that target. Only about 3,000 soldiers would stay in New York. Their main job was to guard the city. If Burgoyne's army made progress toward the Hudson River, the New York force would try to help

The Battle of Trenton was a stunning defeat for the British, and it changed Howe's strategy for 1777.

Burgoyne. Howe's new plan, that the small British force in New York City might help Burgoyne, was very different from the old plan saying that a large force in New York City would definitely help Burgoyne.

In the early months of 1777 no important British leader worried about such a big change in strategy. In New York a British officer wrote, "In spite of all our blunders" the war would be won "before the autumn" of 1777. In London Germain approved of Howe's new strategy. He called it "solid and decisive." Months later people saw that a plan that failed to make sure the two armies cooperated was a bad plan.

The American strategy

After the Battle of Princeton George Washington led his army to Morristown, New Jersey. The army went into winter quarters. Because their terms of enlistment (the amount of time a soldier agreed to serve in the army) had ended, most of the soldiers went home.

Congress had voted to raise a new army to replace the men who went home. But the new soldiers were slow to gather. Washington warned, "The campaign is opening, and we have no men for the field." There were four groups of American soldiers. Washington's small army stayed in New Jersey to watch Howe's army in New York. Another force was in the Hudson Highlands. Their job was to prevent the British from moving north up the Hudson River. Farther north 2,500 Continentals guarded Fort Ticonderoga. In the Mohawk Valley 450 Continentals guarded Fort Stanwix.

The American leaders did not know the British strategy. All they could do was wait for the British to begin their campaign. In other words, the American forces would be on the defensive (defending their positions), while the British would be on the offensive (attacking the Americans).

Decisions in Paris

While British and American leaders made plans for the 1777 campaign, French leaders also thought about the fighting in North America. At that time France was at peace with England. But French leaders still thought of

The British government hired German mercenaries, including Hessian grenadiers, to help them fight the rebels. The Hessians survived their first winter in North America in fine shape because the winter was unusually mild. For years afterward, Canadians spoke of this mild winter as the "German Winter."

the British as their enemies. France and England had fought many wars against one another over the past centuries. In the most recent war, which Americans called the French and Indian War, the British had captured Canada from the French. French leaders wanted revenge.

Back in 1775 it had made French leaders happy when British rebels in America attacked British soldiers. When the campaign of 1776 began with a series of bad American defeats, French leaders asked themselves if the British were close to crushing the rebels.

The French Foreign Minister was Count Charles Vergennes. Vergennes hated England. Vergennes believed that the revolt of the American colonies gave

The French government helped the American rebels in many ways, including allowing American warships such as the Continental navy's *Dolphin* to use French ports.

France a good chance to fight England again. French leaders knew that most of the British army was in America. That made England weaker in other places. Vergennes was making plans for a war when news came about the August 1776 British victory on Long Island (see Volume 4). That news made Vergennes cautious. France could not risk fighting England all by itself. So, instead of helping the American rebels openly, Vergennes thought up a way to help the Americans in secret.

The French set up a fake business called Hortalez and Cie (Company). During the summer of 1776 the French government gave Hortalez and Cie a large amount of money. Vergennes convinced France's old ally, Spain, to send money also. French merchants also loaned money to Hortalez and Cie. On July 18 the company got in touch with the American agent in France, Silas Deane.

Back in April 1776 Deane had sailed from America for France. Congress gave Deane the job of buying supplies for the American army. Congress ordered Deane to work with his old friend, Edward Bancroft. In France Deane and Bancroft set to work. Deane did not know that Bancroft was a British spy! Bancroft passed most of the American and French secrets to the British government.

Still, because of the efforts of Silas Deane and Foreign Minister Vergennes, ships loaded with important supplies, including money, secretly sailed to America. The first big convoy, or group of ships, reached Portsmouth, New Hampshire, in early 1777. It carried 200 field guns (light artillery pieces), thousands of muskets, a large supply of gunpowder, blankets, clothes, and shoes. There were enough supplies to equip 25,000 rebel soldiers.

The news of the rebel victories at Trenton and Princeton encouraged the French to think again about fighting against the British. Vergennes and other leaders began the work of getting France ready for a war. They ordered French warships to be gotten ready to fight the British. Then, French leaders waited to see what would happen in America. The French did not know how much they could count on the Americans to keep fighting. For the French the decision to enter the war against England depended on how well the American rebels fought during 1777.

CHAPTER TWO

The British Invasion Begins

The ship carrying General John Burgoyne from London arrived in Quebec, Canada, on May 6, 1777. Burgoyne met with General Carleton to tell him the news that he, Burgoyne, would take command of the army that was to march south. That news made Carleton angry. Carleton held a higher rank than Burgoyne. He thought that he should command the army. But the orders from London were clear: Carleton was to command only the forces that stayed in Canada; Burgoyne was to command the invasion.

While he was still in London, Burgoyne had written "Thoughts for Conducting the War on the Side of Canada," which described in detail Burgoyne's strategy. Both Germain and the king approved Burgoyne's plan.

The plan called for Carleton to hold Canada with 3,770 men. The main army, numbering 7,173 British and Hessian soldiers, would move up Lake Champlain, capture Fort Ticonderoga, and march to Albany, New York. Meanwhile, a smaller force of about 2,000 men, commanded by Lieutenant Colonel Barry St. Leger, was to sail west along the St. Lawrence River and on to Lake Ontario. St. Leger's force would land at Oswego. Then it would march into the Mohawk River Valley and capture Fort Stanwix. St. Leger's force would continue east and meet Burgoyne at Albany. Some time later Burgoyne's army would cooperate with the British forces in New York City.

Burgoyne found that the army in Canada was in excellent shape. The Hessians were especially healthy because the winter had been unusually mild. Carleton had worked hard to collect supplies and boats. Spies and

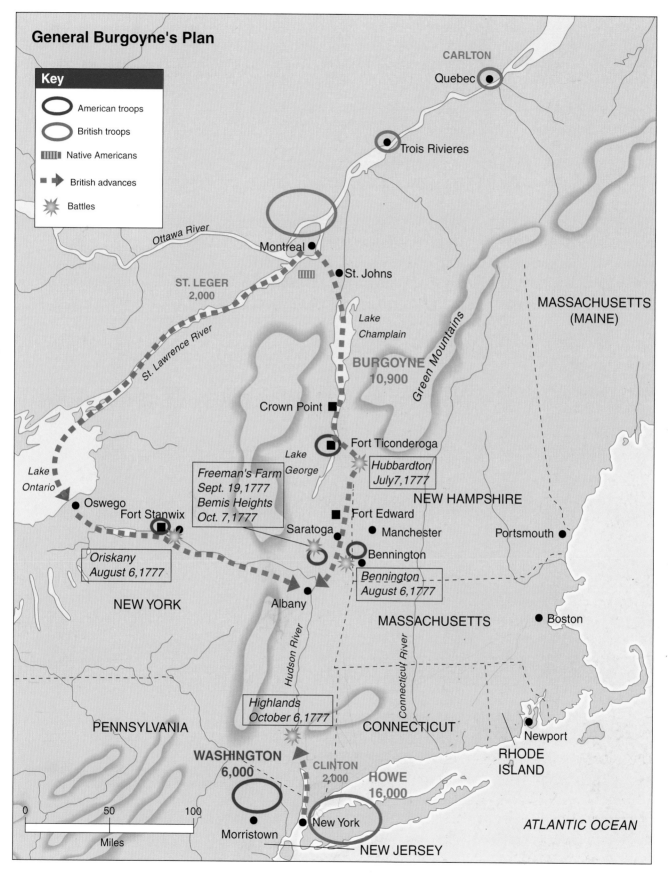

General Burgoyne's Plan

Key

- ⬭ American troops
- ⬭ British troops
- ||||| Native Americans
- ▪▪▶ British advances
- ✸ Battles

CARLTON
Quebec

Trois Rivieres

Ottawa River

Montreal
St. Johns

ST. LEGER
2,000

St. Lawrence River

Lake
Champlain

BURGOYNE
10,900

Green Mountains

MASSACHUSETTS
(MAINE)

Crown Point

Fort Ticonderoga

Lake George

Hubbardton
July 7, 1777

NEW HAMPSHIRE

Freeman's Farm
Sept. 19, 1777
Bemis Heights
Oct. 7, 1777

Lake
Ontario

Oswego
Fort Stanwix

Fort Edward

Saratoga
Manchester

Portsmouth

Oriskany
August 6, 1777

Bennington

Bennington
August 6, 1777

NEW YORK

Albany

MASSACHUSETTS

Boston

Hudson River

Connecticut River

CONNECTICUT

Highlands
October 6, 1777

PENNSYLVANIA

WASHINGTON
6,000

CLINTON
2,000

HOWE
16,000

RHODE
ISLAND

Newport

Morristown

New York

ATLANTIC OCEAN

NEW JERSEY

0   50   100
Miles

scouts reported that the Americans at Fort Ticonderoga were weak. Still, the distance from the Canadian border to Albany and New York via the Hudson River was about 200 miles in a straight line. The army could move along part of the distance by using boats. But the land portion of the journey was through dense forest filled with ancient trees with trunks six feet thick.

Burgoyne faced only three problems that he did not expect. His army needed many wagons and horses. Canadian civilians refused to sell or rent them to the army. So, soldiers had to build 500 new carts out of new, or green, wood. The rough wilderness roads would cause the carts to fall apart. Burgoyne thought that thousands of New York loyalists, or Tories, would join

Burgoyne's army needed hundreds of carts to carry supplies such as gunpowder.

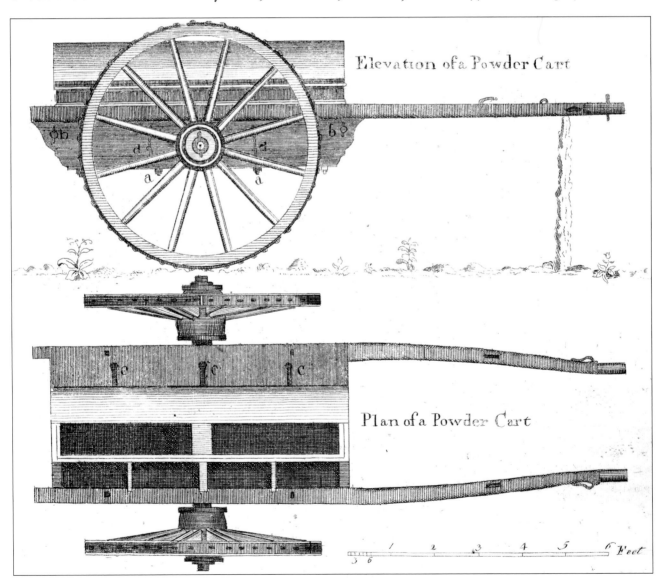

Elevation of a Powder Cart

Plan of a Powder Cart

his army. Instead, only about 100 joined him. Finally, Burgoyne expected that there would be thousands of **Indians** who would serve as his allies.

The Indians

During the French and Indian War (1754-1763) most Native Americans, called Indians by the people living in the British colonies, fought on the French side. They fought to defend their homelands from British settlers. The exceptions were the five tribes in upper New York who formed the Iroquois League. Those five tribes fought on the British side.

When the Revolutionary War began, the Massachusetts Provincial Congress accepted the offer of the Stockbridge Indians to form a company of minutemen. So, the rebel side was the first to use Indians in the Revolution. Then, some rebel leaders tried to encourage other tribes, including the Iroquois, to join the fight. Their efforts did not work.

In May 1775 Congress told its Indian commissioners, the men whose job it was to negotiate with the Indians, to try to convince the Indians to stay out of the war. Congress voted money for rum and gifts to give to the Indians to keep them neutral, or out of the fight. Congress wrote a speech to be read to the Iroquois: "Brothers and friends! . . . This is a family quarrel between us and Old England. You Indians are not concerned in it."

Most Indians did not trust the Americans. They had good reasons for their lack of trust. Americans had been fighting against Indians for more than 100 years. American colonists kept moving west to settle on Indian lands during the Revolutionary War. The Indians knew that if they let it continue, they would lose their land forever.

New Hampshire shared the attitude of most Americans toward the Indians. In 1776 New Hampshire offered the large sum of 70 pounds for each scalp (a section of skin and hair cut off the head of a dead person) of an enemy male Indian. New Hampshire offered about half as much for the scalp of an Indian woman or child.

Because of the mistrust and even hatred between Americans and Indians, Congress's effort to negotiate with the Indians was unlikely to succeed. Also, Congress

An Iroquois chief wears a British army symbol of leadership, called a gorget, hanging below his neck.

INDIANS: the name given to all Native Americans at the time Europeans settled the New World. The name was chosen because the first European explorers thought the New World was part of India.

17

Burgoyne's decision to use Indians led to big problems during his campaign.

was so short of money that it could not pay the Continental soldiers. So, it is no surprise that Congress failed also to find money to buy gifts for the Indians so that negotiations could go smoothly.

British officials thought that the Indians would be very useful allies. The British held a meeting, or council, with the Indians at Oswego, on the southern shore of Lake Ontario. Except for the Oneidas, who lived around the head of the Mohawk Valley, the Iroquois and other Indian tribes agreed to fight for the British.

Because he had served for years in Canada, General Carleton was more experienced with the Indians than Burgoyne. Carleton suggested that Burgoyne not use the Indians. But Burgoyne thought that they would make good scouts. So he decided to include the Indians in his army. However, only about 400 Indians joined Burgoyne's army in Canada. A much larger group joined St. Leger for his advance through the Mohawk Valley.

On June 23, 1777, Burgoyne met with his Indian allies. He gave a speech trying to make them fight humanely (follow the rules of war and not kill and torture prisoners). In part Burgoyne said, "I positively forbid bloodshed" except when they were fighting armed men. "Aged men, women, children and prisoners must be held sacred from the knife or hatchet." The Indians did not like those words. They did not want a British general to tell them what to do. They wanted to fight in the way they had always fought.

Burgoyne also sent a proclamation, or message, to the rebels. He warned, "I have but to give stretch [let go, or release] to the Indian forces under my direction . . . to overtake [and kill] the hardened enemies of Great Britain." In other words, Burgoyne was threatening the rebels, saying he would send the Indians on raids if the Americans refused to give up. Burgoyne's proclamation did not scare the rebels. Instead, it made them mad.

Burgoyne lectured the Indians about the way he expected them to behave. The Indians did not care to be lectured.

Major General Baron Friedrich Riedesel commanded the 3,000 Germans who took part in Burgoyne's campaign.

The Capture of Fort Ticonderoga

From the time Burgoyne arrived in Canada until his army was ready to move, six weeks passed. Finally, Burgoyne told his soldiers, "This Army Must Not Retreat," and ordered the advance to begin. On June 18 Burgoyne's army climbed onto boats and ships and headed south down Lake Champlain. Eyewitnesses, people who were actually there at that time, recalled how the soldiers made a colorful display. There were red-coated British, blue-coated Hessians, and canoes full of Indian allies in war paint. A British lieutenant described the scene:

"We were in the widest part of the lake...the whole army appeared in one view.... In the front the Indians went with their birch canoes, containing twenty or thirty each; then the advanced corps in a regular line, with the gunboats; then followed the *Royal George* and *Inflexible* [larger warships]... after them the first brigade in a regular line; then the Generals Burgoyne, Phillips, and Riedesel [the Hessian general] in their [boats]; next to them were the second brigade, followed by the German brigades; and the rear was brought up with the sutlers and followers of the army [women and servants]."

Burgoyne's force numbered about 10,500 people. That number included about 1,000 people who were not soldiers. They had such duties as driving the wagons and carts and cooking for the officers. The British landed near Fort Ticonderoga on July 1 and prepared to attack the fort. The Indians moved ahead of the British. They kept the Americans from seeing what the British were doing.

The American commander at Fort Ticonderoga was General Arthur St. Clair. During the winter and spring his soldiers had worked hard to build defenses. A young American artist named John Trumbull and a Polish military engineer, Thaddeus Kosciuszko, planned the defenses.

On the west side of the lake was the old Fort Ticonderoga. On the east side was high ground that the rebels named Mount Independence. The Americans fortified (dug trenches and built log and dirt defenses

Because many Americans blamed General Arthur St. Clair for losing Fort Ticonderoga, he was tried by court martial in 1778. The judges decided that St. Clair had not done anything wrong. Still, because St. Clair had been born in Scotland, some people thought that he might be a traitor, or working for the British. For that reason, St. Clair never had another battle command.

Below: Guns at Fort Ticonderoga pointed toward Lake Champlain.

on) Mount Independence. They built a bridge one-quarter mile long to connect the fort with Mount Independence. A barrier of logs and iron chains protected the bridge and blocked British boats from moving past the fort.

The problem for General St. Clair was that his force numbered only about 2,500 men. There were too few to guard all the places that needed guarding. St. Clair knew that a nearby hill that stood 800 feet high, called Mount Defiance, was important. If the British dragged artillery up that hill, the artillery could bombard Fort Ticonderoga. But St. Clair did not have enough men to defend Mount Defiance.

St. Clair hoped that Burgoyne would foolishly attack Fort Ticonderoga. Instead, a British engineer officer suggested to Burgoyne that he move cannons to Mount Defiance. Mount Defiance was steep. Moving guns up the slope would be difficult. British General William Phillips took command of the effort. He said, "Where a goat can go a man can go, and where a man can go he can drag a gun." The British began building a road up Mount Defiance on July 4.

The Americans saw what the British were doing. St. Clair met with his generals. They decided to abandon the fort. St. Clair made excellent plans for the American retreat. One column, or group, moved off to Skenesboro, New York, in boats. The other column was to march overland to join them. The success of the retreat depended on the Americans escaping during the night. They had to move quickly and quietly. The good plan fell apart because of two bad American mistakes.

The rebel commander on Mount Independence was a Frenchman named Matthias Farm. Farm had come to America as a volunteer. He claimed that he was a colonel in the French engineers. That was not true. He fooled Congress, which made him a general. At 3 A.M. on July 6 Farm got ready to retreat from Mount Independence. He had failed to give orders to his men before he went

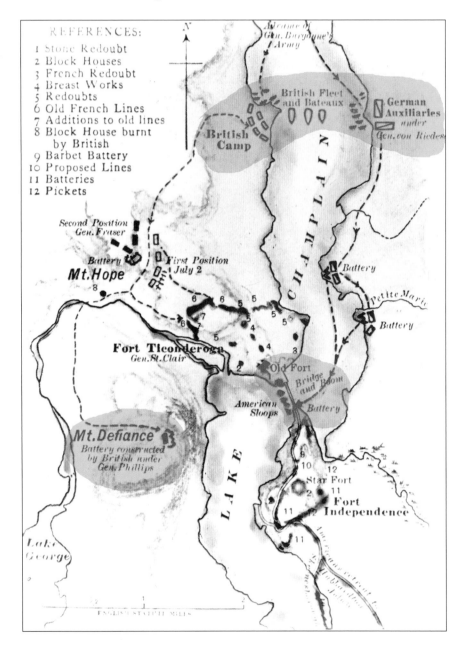

The area around Fort Ticonderoga

to sleep. So, his men did not know what to do. Then, he foolishly set fire to his quarters to keep the British from capturing them.

By the light of the fire the Hessian General Riedesel saw that the Americans were retreating. He sent his men to attack the rebels. The rebel gunners who should have protected the American retreat had gotten drunk and fallen asleep. Their blunder let the Hessians crash through the barrier blocking the lake. The next morning Burgoyne learned that the Americans were retreating. He ordered his men to chase hard after the rebels.

The American officer who commanded the column retreating to Skenesboro, Colonel Pierce Long, thought that the barrier on Lake Champlain would slow the British. So, Long did not hurry to move his own column. Because the British easily moved through the barrier, they almost caught Long. Long and his men had to abandon or burn all their supplies and equipment and run for their lives. The British captured several small American ships and entered the town of Skenesboro.

On July 7 the British continued to chase Long's men. The chase covered twelve miles of forest trail to the gates of an old fort called Fort Anne. The British captured some more rebels who were too sick to move. Early on the morning of July 8 a rebel soldier came to the British camp. He seemed to be a deserter, a soldier who was leaving his army to join the enemy army. The deserter told a British officer that Fort Anne had 1,000 rebel soldiers. He later escaped back to Fort Anne.

The deserter had been a rebel spy. He told the American commander in Fort Anne that the British had only 190 soldiers. The American commander had 400 militia plus the 150 men who had retreated with Colonel Long. The Americans made a fierce attack against the outnumbered British. The British defended a heavily wooded ridge. After two hours it seemed likely that all of the British would be destroyed.

Then soldiers heard an Indian war whoop. It meant that Burgoyne's reinforcements were coming. The Americans retreated, burned Fort Anne, and marched away. In fact, only one British officer arrived as reinforcement. His Indians had refused to join the battle. So, the officer had tried to sound like an Indian in order

A rebel soldier wearing a hunting smock made from undyed material. The loose-fitting smock was much better for marching and fighting in the woods during the summer than the tight-fitting wool uniforms worn by Burgoyne's men.

to scare away the Americans. His war whoop caused the American retreat.

Both sides had used clever tricks in the July 8 Battle of Fort Anne. What was important about such small battles was that the Americans could get more men while Burgoyne could not replace his losses. Every British or Hessian soldier killed or badly wounded was one less soldier who could fight the next battle.

A British soldier who was at Fort Anne wrote:

"It was a distressing sight to see the wounded men bleeding on the ground. . . . The poor fellows [asked] me to tie up their wounds. Immediately I took off my shirt, tore it up, and with the help of a soldier's wife . . . made some bandages, stopped the bleeding of their wounds and [carried] them in blankets to a small hut."

While the British chased Long's column, the second American column that was retreating from Fort Ticonderoga also faced problems. General St. Clair had hoped to join Long at Skenesboro. He had a difficult march because the trail was steep, and the day was very hot. St. Clair led most of his men through a two-house settlement named Hubbardton. Seth Warner, the officer who had taken command of the Green Mountain Boys, was left behind to collect the men who had not been able to keep up. Warner did not follow orders. Instead of collecting the men and moving on, he camped that night at Hubbardton. Warner failed to set out guards.

A British column commanded by General Simon Fraser had left Lake Champlain at 4 A.M. on July 6. It spent the day marching fast toward the rebels. A Hessian column commanded by Riedesel followed Fraser. The two generals agreed to attack the Americans on July 7. The British and Hessian soldiers advanced at 3 A.M. on July 7. Because the Americans did not have guards protecting them, the British caught the Americans eating breakfast. They routed the rebels and charged ahead.

A bloody two-hour fight took place. A British major stepped onto a tree stump to look at the American position. An American rifleman shot him dead. The British General Fraser was close to losing when the Hessians arrived. Riedesel ordered his Hessians to sing while the band played in order to encourage the British. His idea worked. The British and Hessians drove the rebels from the field and captured many prisoners and 12 cannons. Seth Warner gave the last order to the American side: "Scatter and meet me at Manchester."

Before and during the Revolutionary War people thought that Fort Ticonderoga was a very important place. The British had easily captured Fort Ticonderoga. Then, they had won two small victories at Skenesboro and Hubbardton. Those events discouraged the rebels. Many blamed St. Clair. He had ordered the fort abandoned without a fight. An American doctor wrote, "This disaster has given to our cause a dark and gloomy [look]." The doctor added that St. Clair is "very unpopular."

While the capture of Ticonderoga discouraged the rebels, it encouraged the British. Burgoyne was always confident. His success made him even more confident. Because the rebels had failed to defend the fort, he said that the rebels "have no men of military science." He believed that his army could beat the rebels at any place and at any time.

When the news about Fort Ticonderoga came to London, King George rushed to tell the queen, "I have beat them! I have beat all the Americans!"

An American rifleman. The word "liberty" is written on his helmet.

25

CHAPTER THREE

Burgoyne Makes a Mistake

General Howe stayed in New York City until he learned that Burgoyne had captured Fort Ticonderoga. That news seemed to prove that Burgoyne's campaign was going well. So, Howe ordered his army to board their ships and sail south to attack Philadelphia. That decision agreed with the British plan that had been worked out in the winter. But it meant that Howe would not be in a position to help Burgoyne if Burgoyne got into trouble.

The American commander of the Northern Department, Philip Schuyler

George Washington did not know where Howe might go. The British control of the sea gave the British a huge advantage. British ships could take British infantry anywhere along the American coast. American infantry would have to march to meet the British, and that would take them a long time. Meanwhile, Washington knew that the American commander in the north, General Philip Schuyler, needed help.

Washington could not spare very much. Howe's army outnumbered Washington's army. But Washington did send Daniel Morgan and his riflemen north to join Schuyler. Washington also ordered two brigades of Continentals to move from Peekskill, New York, to Albany. He also sent the fiery Benedict Arnold to join Schuyler. Congress urged the governors of New York and New England to recruit more Continentals and to call out the militia. Last, Washington had General Benjamin Lincoln go to Vermont to organize and command the New England militia.

The American commander in the north (the Northern Department) was Philip Schuyler. The Schuyler family had come to America when the Dutch settled New York. They were a proud and rich family. When Congress started naming men to be generals in 1775, it chose Philip Schuyler as the number-three major general. Only Washington and two other generals held higher rank than Schuyler.

Schuyler had taken part in the American invasion of Canada in 1776. At that time a problem with Schuyler's personality emerged. Schuyler treated common soldiers like

Burgoyne's march to the Hudson River

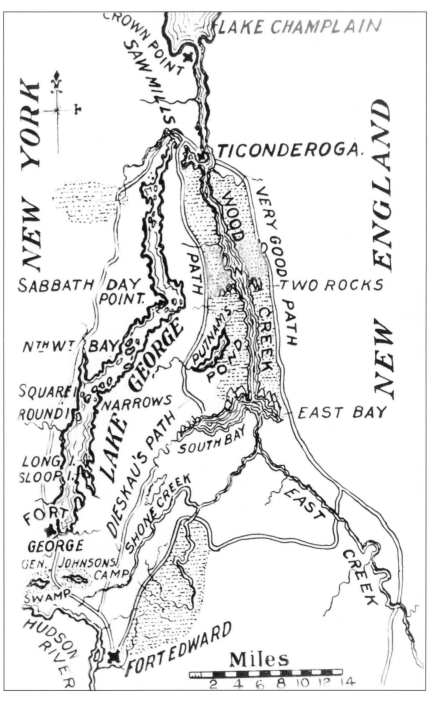

servants. He was used to giving orders and having men obey them. He was strict in everything to do with discipline. Most of his soldiers were from New England. The New Englanders did not like the way Schuyler treated them. They complained to their congressmen about Schuyler.

While Congress thought about replacing Schuyler, Burgoyne thought about what to do next. The direct route to Albany was along Lake George. A wagon road ran along the lake. But Burgoyne worried that the rebels would build a fleet on Lake George to block the route. So, he chose another route that went from Skenesboro and followed a river called Wood Creek. That route was a narrow forest trail that led to Fort Edward on the Hudson River. When Burgoyne chose the Wood Creek route, he made a big mistake.

Schuyler ordered a force of 1,000 men to take axes and cut trees across the trail. In swampy places the rebel workers dug ditches so that water flowed onto the trail. They rolled big rocks into Wood Creek to keep boats from using the river.

A blockhouse on the hill overlooks a loyalist's saw mill, used to make lumber for the British march along Wood Creek.

It took the British 20 days to move 22 miles. They had to build 40 bridges. In one swampy section the British built a raised road, or causeway, two miles long. On July 29 the British finally reached Fort Edward. Meanwhile, another British force found that the Americans had not built a fleet on Lake George. The force cleared the lake and captured Fort George.

Burgoyne had reached the Hudson River. If he had moved right away, his army could have captured Albany. But he did not have enough supplies to march to Albany. His army stood at the end of a supply line that stretched 185 miles back to Montreal, Canada. Everything the British army needed had to move along this line. Burgoyne remembered Bunker Hill. He did not want to fight the rebels without the help of his artillery. So, he ordered 52 cannons moved forward. That would take time. Meanwhile, the army was still short of horses to haul the carts and wagons needed to carry supplies. A force of 250 Brunswick cavalry (German troops) had no horses at all.

The German General Riedesel suggested that a force

Patriots were willing to destroy their own property to keep the British from getting food and supplies. The wife of General Philip Schuyler sets her family's cornfield on fire as the British approach.

raid into the Connecticut Valley to the east because reports said that there were horses and supplies in this valley. Burgoyne liked the idea but made some changes. Because the Americans had failed to defend Fort Ticonderoga, Burgoyne did not respect the rebel leaders and their soldiers. In other words, he was overconfident. He ordered Riedesel to raid deep into rebel territory. Riedesel argued that it was too dangerous. Burgoyne did not listen.

At that time very few people lived in Vermont. So, Vermont leaders called on New Hampshire and Massachusetts for help. New Hampshire was already organizing its militia to fight Burgoyne. On July 17 John Stark, one of the heroes of the Battle of Bunker Hill (see Volume 2), stepped forward to command the militia. He was so popular that within one week he had raised 1,492 officers and men. By July 30 Stark's men were marching to Manchester, New Hampshire. Around that time they heard the news that Burgoyne's Indian allies had done something terrible.

A 6-pound howitzer, one of the types of artillery used by both the British and American armies

The Killing of Jane McCrea

During the campaign so far, Burgoyne's Indian allies had not done much to help the British. During the time the Americans were cutting down trees to block the British advance, the Indians had done little to stop them. Instead, the Indians went ahead of the army to raid. Sometimes they attacked American soldiers. For example, on July 21 the Indians surrounded 34 rebel scouts belonging to the 7th Massachusetts Regiment. They killed all but 12 of the Massachusetts men. The next day Indians killed a rebel guard and scalped another soldier. The 7th Massachusetts fought the Indians for 30 minutes. By the end of the battle eight more Massachusetts men were dead and 15 wounded.

Burgoyne's Indians terrified the rebels. A man carries a dying woman who has been struck by an arrow in her back.

Burgoyne had planned on having the Indians frighten the Americans so badly that they would stop fighting against his army. His plan seemed to be working. The Americans in the Hudson Valley around Albany lived in terror. It seemed to them that Schuyler and his army could do nothing to protect them.

Schuyler's army had grown to about 4,500 men, but many of them were scared and discouraged. A growing number of men were deserting the rebel army. Then, just before Burgoyne's army reached the Hudson River, the Indians did something that caused big problems for the British.

Jane McCrea was a young woman who lived with her brother on the Hudson River. She was engaged to

Patriot writers used the killing of Jane McCrea to inspire Americans to fight for the rebel cause.

Lieutenant David Jones, a Tory who was serving with Burgoyne's army. She traveled to Fort Edward, where she hoped to meet up with Jones. She was staying with an elderly woman near the fort on July 27, 1777, when a band of Indians appeared. The Indians were far in front of the British army. They captured the two women and carried them into the forest.

When the Indians rejoined the British army, one Indian carried a long-haired woman's scalp tied to his belt. Lieutenant Jones recognized that it was Jane McCrea's scalp. Exactly how and why the Indians killed McCrea is unknown. Burgoyne knew that if he punished the Indians, they would go back to Canada. So he did nothing.

The news of the killing of Jane McCrea spread to the rebel side. American leaders skillfully used the story to make people angry at the British. The *New York Gazette* and *Weekly Mercury* published the sensational news about the killing of Jane McCrea on August 11. The next day the *Pennsylvania Evening Post* published the news. On August 14 it appeared in the *Massachusetts Spy* and in the *Maryland Gazette*. Two days later the *New Hampshire Gazette* published the story. By August 22 the news had reached Virginia.

The news aroused the Americans. New York and New England men flocked to join the militia. They wanted revenge for the death of Jane McCrea. They also wanted to defend their homes because they knew that British forces were approaching. It was as if Burgoyne's use of Indians to terrorize the rebels had stirred up a hornet's nest. Now, the angry hornets were getting ready to sting.

The Bennington Raid

When John Stark's men reached Manchester, they met up with the Vermonters who served with Seth Warner. Warner's last order at the Battle of Hubbardton (July 7, 1777) had been "Scatter and meet me at Manchester." Some of Warner's men obeyed his order. Also at Manchester was General Benjamin Lincoln, the officer

George Washington sent General Benjamin Lincoln to help raise the New England militia against Burgoyne.

whom George Washington had ordered to help command rebel forces in the north.

Lincoln held a higher rank than Stark. But Stark refused to take orders from Lincoln. Lincoln could have made a fuss about Stark's behavior. Instead, he wisely let Stark suggest what to do. Stark wanted to raid against Burgoyne's long supply line. Lincoln told Stark to go ahead. That decision proved important because it placed Stark in a position to fight against the German forces moving toward Bennington.

A Brunswick lieutenant colonel named Friedrich Baum commanded the British raiding force. It was a strange force. The column hoped to attract many loyalists. Yet, Baum spoke no English, which made it hard for him to communicate. Baum's men needed to march quickly, yet there were 170 dismounted cavalrymen in the column. The cavalrymen wore high boots designed for riding horses. They gave the men painful blisters when they had to walk. Baum's men hoped to march secretly and surprise the rebels. Yet, a German band was among the column.

Baum's column approached Bennington on August 14, 1777. Baum had learned that there were many valuable supplies at Bennington. He wanted to capture the supplies. Baum had thought that there were only 300 to 400 militia in Bennington. On August 14 he found out that there were many more rebels there. He sent a messenger asking for reinforcements. He then halted to wait for the reinforcements. The messenger arrived at Burgoyne's headquarters before dawn on August 15. Burgoyne chose the German grenadiers commanded by Lieutenant Colonel Heinrich Breymann to march the 25 miles and join Baum. That too was a bad decision because the German grenadiers were not used to moving quickly.

Meanwhile, General John Stark was in Bennington with his New Hampshire troops. Many militia, angry about the death of Jane McCrea, joined Stark's men at Bennington. On August 16 Stark led them in an attack against Baum's Germans. Stark shouted out to his men, "We'll beat them before night, or Molly Stark will be a widow."

For two hours a fierce fight took place. Some of Baum's men ran away. A Tory wrote: "I saw all my

A Brunswick dragoon, one of the German troops, wearing his riding boots.

companions were going over the wall...and I went too....I ran some distance with another man, and looking around saw several...soldiers who were coming after us....We had just reached a rail fence, and both of us gave a jump at the same instant to go over it. While I was in the air, I heard the guns go off. We reached the ground together, but my companion fell and lay dead by the fence, while I ran on with all my might."

Most of the Germans fought well. But Stark's men almost managed to surround them. The German cavalry, still fighting on foot, drew their long swords. Baum

The Battle of Bennington, August 16, 1777

A Hessian grenadier begs for mercy from an American militiaman.

bravely led them in a charge. Stark's militia had no bayonets to fight against the swords. The rebels were moving back when someone shot Baum in the stomach. It was a mortal wound. Baum's loss discouraged his men, and they surrendered.

Near the end of the battle the German reinforcements, grenadiers commanded by Breymann, arrived. Their arrival surprised the Americans, who thought that they had already won the battle and had scattered around the battlefield. Stark considered ordering a retreat. But he too had received reinforcements. Seth Warner joined him with about 350 men. Warner urged Stark to stay and fight. Then Breymann's grenadiers charged, and a second battle took place.

Both sides stood firm and fired at each other. Near sunset Breymann's men ran low on ammunition. Breymann ordered a retreat. Even though he was wounded, Breymann personally commanded the rear guard that covered the retreat. Two-thirds of Breymann's men escaped. Stark later said, "Had the day lasted an hour longer, we should have taken the whole [group]."

The Battle of Bennington was a confused and amazing battle. About 2,000 American militia, most of whom were farmers, had badly beaten German professional soldiers. The Americans lost about 14 killed and 42 wounded. The Germans left some 207 dead on the

The German Colonel Baum's wound discouraged his men.

battlefield along with several hundred muskets and four cannons. The Americans captured 700 prisoners. John Stark had shown superb leadership. Congress later rewarded him by making him a brigadier general in the Continental army.

The Americans captured about 700 prisoners at the Battle of Bennington.

The patriot victory at the Battle of Bennington came at an important time. After a series of defeats the victory again encouraged the Americans. The battle was a disaster for Burgoyne. It left his army still short of supplies. It also subtracted more than ten percent from Burgoyne's strength.

CHAPTER FOUR

The Campaign for the Mohawk Valley

While Burgoyne's army was moving south toward the Hudson River, another British force was invading the Mohawk Valley. Lieutenant-Colonel Barry St. Leger commanded the force. His mission was to attract, or divert, American attention away from Burgoyne. St. Leger's force included about 1,000 Indians, 340 regular soldiers, and 360 Tory and Canadian men.

On July 25 St. Leger's little army reached Oswego. The next day, at the time Burgoyne was almost to the Hudson, it left Oswego on a march toward Fort Stanwix. The advance had to go through a wilderness. Still, St. Leger made good progress, averaging about ten miles each day. His army reached Fort Stanwix on August 2.

Inside the fort were 750 Americans commanded by Colonel Peter Gansevoort of New York. Most of the defenders belonged to the 3rd New York Continentals. They had worked hard to prepare the fort for a battle. St. Leger saw that he could not charge, or assault, the fort. Instead, he tried to bluff the Americans by gathering his army within their sight and then demanding that Gansevoort surrender.

St. Leger's bluff backfired. The fort's defenders saw St. Leger's powerful force of Indians. They feared that they would be slaughtered by the Indians if they surrendered. So, the defenders decided to fight hard to hold the fort. St. Leger had no choice but to begin a **siege**. On the evening of August 5 St. Leger learned that another

Lieutenant-Colonel Barry St. Leger commanded the British force that invaded the Mohawk Valley.

SIEGE: a campaign to capture a place by surrounding it, cutting it off from supplies, and attacking it cautiously under the cover of trenches and earthworks

40

The Mohawk war chief Thayendanegea, known to the whites as Joseph Brant, fought in his first battle at the age of thirteen. He went on to become one of the greatest Indian leaders.

American force was marching to reinforce Fort Stanwix. He sent 400 Indians commanded by a remarkable Mohawk leader named Thayendanegea, or Joseph Brant to the whites, to ambush the Americans.

A militia officer named Nicholas Herkimer commanded the American force. When he had heard that St. Leger was getting close, Herkimer quickly gathered a force of 800 militia. He set out to relieve, or save, Fort Stanwix. On August 6 the militia were crossing a wide ravine when the Indians opened fire at very close range. Many American officers fell at the first shots. Some of the militia broke and ran in terror.

Herkimer received a bad leg wound. He calmly propped himself against a tree, smoked his pipe, and continued to direct the rebel militia. His courage inspired the New York militia. At first the militia fought as individuals. The Indians waited until a militiaman fired his musket, and then they charged to kill him before he could reload.

The wounded General Nicholas Herkimer, holding his pipe, directs his soldiers at the Battle of Oriskany.

Herkimer organized the militia into pairs of fighters. While one man reloaded, the other held his fire (waited with loaded gun) to prevent the Indians from coming close. A hard six-hour fight took place.

The August 6 fight became known as the Battle of Oriskany. Both sides lost heavily. Herkimer's militia took so many casualties that they retreated away from Fort Stanwix. While the fight was taking place, back at Fort Stanwix a smart American officer named Marinus Willet led a rebel raid against the Indian camp. Willet's men stole all of the Indian's possessions, including blankets, packs, and ammunition, and carried them back inside Fort Stanwix. When Thayendanegea's warriors returned from their battle, they were angry to see what had happened.

St. Leger had promised the Indians that they would not have to fight very much and that they would collect lots of valuable items from the rebels. Instead, the Indians had taken heavy losses in the campaign's first battle and had lost all of their possessions. The Indians felt as though St. Leger had lied to them.

News of the Battle of Oriskany reached General Schuyler quickly. The first report said that Herkimer's army had been "cut to pieces." Schuyler was in a difficult situation. Burgoyne's army was only 24 miles away. But Schuyler figured that he had time to send help to Fort Stanwix before Burgoyne advanced farther.

Schuyler's New England officers argued against Schuyler's plan. The New Englanders neither liked nor trusted the New Yorker Schuyler. They accused Schuyler of neglecting New England's defense in order to protect

Bitter hand-to-hand fighting at the Battle of Oriskany, August 6, 1777

Benedict Arnold

Benedict Arnold, born in Connecticut in 1741, was actually Benedict Arnold V. The first Benedict Arnold had been governor of Rhode Island colony in the 1650s. Arnold was one of six children. Only Benedict and one sister lived through the epidemics that killed the other four children.

After Benedict's brothers and sisters died, his father began to drink too much alcohol and became unable to work. The successful family business failed, and Benedict had to leave school because his father could no longer pay for it. Benedict became an apprentice to a druggist at the age of 15. He soon impressed his employer with his intelligence and business sense.

By the time Arnold was 21 years old, his parents had died. Arnold moved to another town and opened a shop that sold medicines and books. His former employer loaned him money to get started. Arnold was determined to restore his family's reputation, which had been damaged by his father's drinking and loss of his business.

Benedict Arnold became very successful in business. He bought trading ships and went on voyages to buy and sell horses, rum, molasses, and timber. He married in 1767, and he and his wife had three sons. Yet the embarrassments of his youth stayed with him, and he was always sensitive about what people thought of him.

Arnold was one of the first people in his town to support the patriot cause. He left a thriving business, growing family, and fine home to organize a company of militia and join the Revolution. His wife would die while he was off at war. His company elected him as their captain in December 1774. So Benedict Arnold began the military career that found him a major general at the Battle of Saratoga.

New York's Mohawk Valley. Schuyler said that he would take personal responsibility for sending reinforcements to Fort Stanwix and called for a brigadier general to command the effort. Benedict Arnold volunteered.

Arnold led a force of about 950 Continentals. Bad

roads slowed the march. Arnold also had to pause to wait for militia reinforcements. However, after the Battle of Oriskany the militia had lost their desire to fight. Only about 100 militia joined Arnold. Arnold learned that St. Leger's men had dug trenches to within 150 yards of Fort Stanwix. The fort seemed doomed. One of Arnold's officers suggested a trick to help save the fort.

The rebels held a Tory prisoner named Hon Yost. Yost was mentally challenged; people called him crazy or a halfwit. But the Indians often respected people like Yost. They believed that such people had special gifts. The Americans told Yost to go among St. Leger's Indians and tell them that a huge American force was moving to crush the British outside of Fort Stanwix. The Americans kept Yost's brother as a prisoner, or hostage, to make sure that Yost did not betray them.

Yost did his duty with great cunning and skill. The Indians were already tired of fighting for St. Leger. Yost's story convinced them to go home. When his Indian allies deserted him, St. Leger decided to retreat. Arnold and his reinforcements reached Fort Stanwix on August 23. Arnold left a garrison of 700 men to guard the fort and returned to join Schuyler with 1,200 men. Meanwhile, St. Leger retreated back the way he had come.

By the time Arnold returned to the Hudson River, Schuyler no longer commanded the army. The loss of Fort Ticonderoga gave Schuyler's enemies a chance to remove him from command. On August 4, 1777, Schuyler's enemies convinced Congress to appoint a new general. Congress chose General Horatio Gates to replace Schuyler. Gates arrived to take command on August 19. Schuyler acted like a true patriot. He accepted the change. He stayed with the army to help Gates and did important and good work.

Gates found that his 4,000-man army was divided into three parts. Most of his men were at the junction of the Hudson and Mohawk rivers. Arnold was 110 miles to the west at Fort Stanwix. Thirty miles to the east were the soldiers who had won the Battle of Bennington. However, because of the killing of Jane McCrea the militia were gathering quickly. Day by day the Americans were growing stronger. Gates decided to wait and see what Burgoyne did next.

Because New Englanders disliked Schuyler, New England congressmen persuaded Congress in August 1777 to send General Horatio Gates to take command of the Northern Department.

CHAPTER FIVE

The Battle of Freeman's Farm

The two British defeats at Bennington and in the Mohawk Valley weakened Burgoyne's army. More bad news came when Burgoyne learned that General Carleton, back in Canada, was not planning to help him. Carleton had not liked it when Burgoyne took command of the invasion army. Now, he got revenge by refusing to send reinforcements to Burgoyne. So, Burgoyne had to send 900 of his own men back to Fort Ticonderoga to serve as the garrison, or guards, of the fort.

At that point a wise move would have been for Burgoyne to retreat. But he was not the kind of general to do such a thing. If he retreated, he would have to admit that he had failed. Instead, he slowly collected supplies from Canada until he had enough to last his army for 30 days. Then he prepared to advance across the Hudson River and capture Albany.

Burgoyne knew that as soon as he advanced, the Americans around Bennington would attack his supply line somewhere between the Hudson River and Fort Ticonderoga. He also knew that he did not have enough soldiers to guard his supply line. So, he made the bold decision to abandon his supply line.

The advance across the Hudson was a risky move. The army would be unable to find supplies on the west side of the Hudson. To survive, it would have to get supplies from New York City. The supplies would have to move all the way up the Hudson River past the American forces in the Hudson Highlands and past Gates's army

Sometimes American frontiersmen practiced their skills by attending "rifle frolics," events where they competed in target shooting. Gates's army benefitted from having some experienced frontiersmen in its ranks.

The Polish engineer Thaddeus Kosciuszko was a professional military man. He gave Gates expert advice and helped design the fortifications that were a key part of the American position at Saratoga.

near Albany. That would only be possible if Burgoyne defeated Gates, and the British forces in New York City cleared the Hudson Highlands. Everything would have to go right for all of those things to happen. In war everything seldom goes right. In the words of a modern British military historian, for Burgoyne "to advance was folly."

On September 13 Burgoyne, with about 6,000 men, crossed the Hudson River near Saratoga. By that time all but 50 of Burgoyne's Indian allies had left. Although the Indians had caused Burgoyne many problems, they still had been useful as scouts. Without the Indians Burgoyne had very little idea about what lay in front of his army.

Gates's American army included experienced frontiersmen who were good at scouting in the wilderness. They told Gates where Burgoyne was going. The day before Burgoyne crossed the Hudson, Gates moved his army to a position near Stillwater. There it occupied strong defensive ground at Bemis Heights. The Polish engineer Kosciuszko and Benedict Arnold had planned the defense carefully. The position on Bemis Heights blocked Burgoyne's advance to Albany.

While Gates blocked Burgoyne, another American force struck Burgoyne's rear. After the Battle of Bennington General Lincoln had continued to collect militia. Lincoln sent 1,500 militia on a raid toward Fort Ticonderoga. The militia surprised the 900 British soldiers who were guarding the fort and its outposts. They freed 100 American prisoners and captured 300 British.

The rebel raiders safely returned to Vermont. They had learned that Burgoyne's army had enough food for only four weeks. A messenger carried the news to Gates. By the time the messenger reached Gates, the Battle of Freeman's Farm had been fought.

Freeman's Farm

After crossing the Hudson River, Burgoyne moved slowly down the west bank of the river. Without the Indians the British did not have useful scouts. Because trees covered most of the land, it was hard for the British

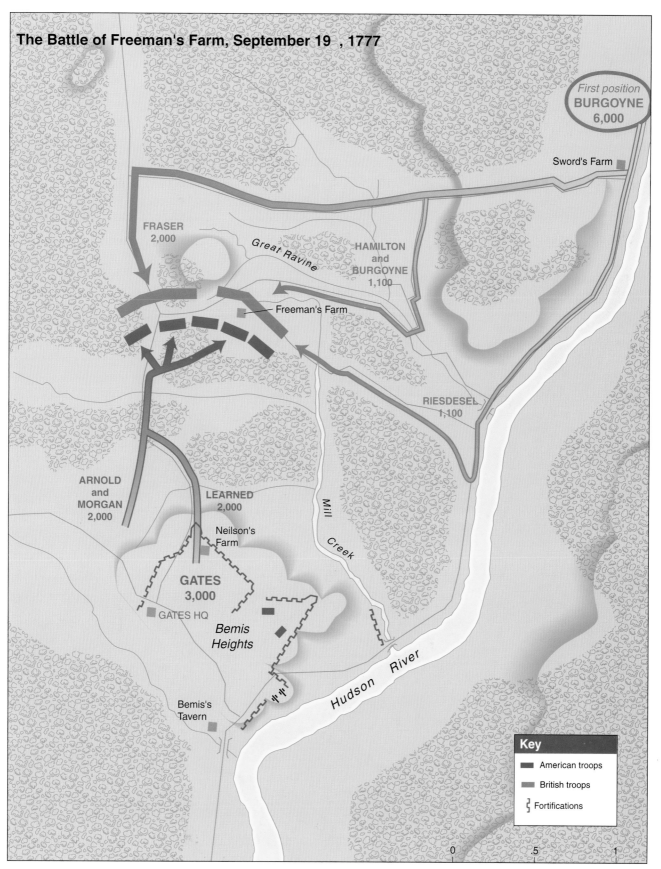

The Battle of Freeman's Farm, September 19 , 1777

First position
BURGOYNE
6,000

Sword's Farm

FRASER
2,000

Great Ravine

HAMILTON
and
BURGOYNE
1,100

Freeman's Farm

RIESDESEL
1,100

ARNOLD
and
MORGAN
2,000

LEARNED
2,000

Mill

Creek

Neilson's
Farm

GATES
3,000

GATES HQ

*Bemis
Heights*

Hudson River

Bemis's
Tavern

Key
■ American troops
■ British troops
⌇ Fortifications

0   5   1

to see what was ahead of them. On September 16 the British heard the sound of beating drums from the high ground in front of them. In that way they learned that they had bumped into the American army.

Burgoyne spent two days getting his army into position. He still did not know exactly where the Americans were. So, he ordered a strong force to advance to locate the rebel position. Burgoyne divided his force into three columns. General Simon Fraser led 2,200 men on the British right. Fraser's mission was to explore a clearing known as Freeman's Farm. Burgoyne moved with the center column, which numbered about

Gates's camp at the Neilson Farm. Gates did not want to move the American army from its camp because the camp was defended by fortifications and was on top of Bemis Heights.

1,100 men. The center column hoped to meet Fraser's men at Freeman's Farm. The German General Riedesel commanded the left column with 1,100 men. Riedesel's mission was to move along the Hudson River.

September 19, 1777, dawned cold and foggy. Burgoyne waited for the fog to clear. Then, around 11 A.M. a British cannon fired. It was the signal for all three columns to advance. By 12:30 the center column reached a small log cabin in the middle of the cleared land of Freeman's Farm. There it waited for the other columns to arrive.

American scouts had seen the British leave their camp. They reported the news to General Gates. Gates considered what to do. His army numbered about 7,000 men. It was in a strong position in trenches on high ground. Gates cautiously decided not to move. Benedict Arnold thought that this decision was a mistake. He said that if the Americans simply sat tight, the British would move around the American left flank. Rather than let that happen, Arnold proposed that the rebels make an attack. After much argument Gates told Arnold to take a small force including Morgan's Virginia riflemen and Henry Dearborn's Continental Light Infantry to fight the British.

Morgan's riflemen reached the edge of Freeman's Farm about 12:45. They carefully aimed their rifles at a group of British officers who were at the cabin in the middle of the open field. Their first shots killed or wounded most of the officers. Their accurate long-range fire discouraged the British, and they ran to the rear. Morgan's men foolishly chased the British.

At close range and in the open the British had the advantage. They had bayonets. Morgan's men did not. The British fought off the riflemen. This time it was the riflemen who ran. The riflemen got back to the safety of the trees. Morgan thought that his unit had been destroyed. He sounded his turkey call, an instrument hunters used to make a sound like a turkey. It was the signal for the riflemen to rally. When the Virginians heard Morgan's call, they rallied around him.

Henry Dearborn commanded the Continental Light Infantry at Freeman's Farm. Dearborn fought in many battles, beginning with Bunker Hill.

Daniel Morgan's Rifles

Daniel Morgan's childhood remains mysterious. He did not talk about his past, and his ancestors are not known to history. Morgan was born around 1735, probably in New Jersey, to poor immigrants from Wales, in Great Britain. His father was most likely a farm laborer. Morgan argued with his father and left home when he was about 18 years old. After working at assorted jobs, he ended up in the frontier town of Winchester, Virginia. He found a job as a driver of wagons, carrying farm produce to market. Soon he saved up enough money to buy his own wagon and team.

When the French and Indian War began, Daniel Morgan first used his wagon to haul ammunition for the British. He helped remove wounded British soldiers after Braddock's defeat in an ambush on the way to Fort Duquesne. Morgan then joined a Virginia militia company. There is a legend that he was severely whipped as punishment for getting into a fight with a British soldier, and that he never forgave the British army. After the war he resumed operating his hauling business. Between hauling trips Morgan played cards, drank, and got into fights with his friends. He eventually settled down and got married. He and his wife, the daughter of a prosperous farmer, had two daughters. By the time the Revolution began, Morgan owned a Virginia farm and ten slaves.

In June 1775 Daniel Morgan was elected captain of one of the companies of "expert riflemen" called for by the Continental Congress. Men of the frontier in western Virginia had the reputation of being excellent marksmen. Morgan's company dressed in buckskin hunting clothes and moccasins. Each man carried a rifle, tomahawk, and scalping knife. Morgan's job was to recruit the riflemen

Daniel Morgan

and march them to Boston. In Boston he volunteered his company for Benedict Arnold's invasion of Canada, and Arnold put Morgan in charge of three rifle companies.

In honor of his brave service in Canada Morgan received promotion to colonel. He took command of a corps of light infantry. This corps included specially picked men from the western frontiers of several states, including Virginia. The men dressed in buckskin hunting dress as had Morgan's original company. Morgan's corps gained a reputation for their ability to take cover and fight in the woods. Morgan used a turkey call to signal his men. When Burgoyne and the British army invaded New York state in 1777, citizens began to call for Morgan's men to be sent to them: "Oh for some Virginia riflemen!" said one.

General Fraser could not tell what his men were up against. The British had captured an American officer. Fraser asked him to tell about the American position. The rebel officer simply said that the army was commanded by Generals Gates and Arnold. His answer made Fraser angry. A British soldier reported,

"General Fraser... told him if he did not immediately inform him as to the exact [American] situation... he would hang him.... The officer, with the most undaunted firmness, replied, 'You may, if you please.' The General, [seeing] he could [learn] nothing ... rode off."

Both sides received reinforcements. But the British were in the open, while the Americans were in the trees on the edge of the field. That gave the rebels an advantage. The American officer James Wilkinson was at the fight. Wilkinson wrote, "The fire of our marksmen from this wood was too deadly to be withstood by the enemy; and when they gave way and broke, our men rushing from [the trees] pursued them ... they rallied; and, charging in turn, drove us back into the wood—from whence a dreadful fire would

American marksmen fire from the shelter of the trees while the British are exposed in the open fields.

again force them to fall back. And in this manner did the battle [flow back and forth], like waves of a stormy sea."

A British soldier described what it was like to be out in the open field: "A constant blaze of fire was kept up, and both armies seemed to be determined on death or victory. . . . Men, and particularly officers, dropped every moment on each side. Several of the Americans [these were Morgan's riflemen] placed themselves in high trees, and as often as they could distinguish a British officer's uniform," the Americans shot at the officer.

The fighting continued for hours. Finally, General Riedesel led his column to help the British at Freeman's Farm. Burgoyne ordered his forces to attack again. The Americans slowly retreated, and darkness came.

The British lost about 600 men during the battle. The Americans lost 319: 8 officers and 57 men killed; 21 officers and 197 men wounded, and 36 missing. Because he held the ground, Burgoyne claimed a victory. But it was only a victory if it accomplished something.

The British could hardly see the American marksmen who were hidden in the tree line.

Perhaps, if Burgoyne had attacked again the next day, he would have driven the tired Americans from Bemis Heights. But General Fraser argued that his soldiers needed to rest for a day. So, Burgoyne decided to wait before attacking again.

On the American side Gates had shown very little leadership. He kept most of his army back on Bemis Heights while a portion of his army fought the battle. If Gates had sent his entire army into battle, the rebels probably would have badly defeated Burgoyne. Once again Arnold showed great energy and bravery during the battle.

Burgoyne was ready to attack on September 21. Then he received a letter from General Clinton, the British commander in New York City. Clinton said that he was moving up the Hudson River toward the Hudson Highlands. This information persuaded Burgoyne to cancel his attack and wait for more news from Clinton. An American historian says, ". . . and by that decision [Burgoyne] lost the last chance for success."

On August 21 the messenger carrying the news of the American raid against Fort Ticonderoga reached Gates. The messenger reported the news that Burgoyne's army had food for only another four weeks. That information helped Gates make his strategy. That night the Americans loudly celebrated the success of the raid. Gates also freed a British prisoner to carry the news to the British army. It was bad news for the British. It told them that their army was cut off from any retreat. At that point Burgoyne concluded that his only hope rested with the moves of General Clinton.

Rebel soldiers gathered around their campfires to celebrate news of the successful raid against Burgoyne's supply line.

CHAPTER SIX

Decision at Saratoga

It was hard for Burgoyne and Clinton to exchange messages. One British messenger carried this secret note from Clinton to Burgoyne in the metal ball at the bottom of the picture. When the rebels captured him, he swallowed it. The rebels forced him to drink something that made him cough it up. Then the rebels hanged the messenger.

When General William Howe took an army to attack Philadelphia, he left Sir Henry Clinton back in New York City. Clinton commanded a force of about 6,900 infantry. Three thousand of them were new loyalist recruits not yet ready for battle. Most of Clinton's force had to serve as guards to defend the city and harbor. So, Clinton decided not to budge and to stay in New York City.

Then, on July 30 Clinton received a letter from Howe. It suggested that Clinton could attack the Hudson Highlands in order to attract rebel attention away from Burgoyne. Clinton doubted that was necessary. Next, he received a letter from Burgoyne on August 6. Burgoyne wrote that everything was going well. More than a month later, on September 11, Clinton learned about the British defeat at Bennington. That news caused Clinton to change his mind. He sent a letter to Burgoyne saying that he would make an attack against the Highlands. But this was not a rescue effort. It was simply a feint, an effort to attract rebel forces away from Burgoyne.

On September 29 Clinton received another message from Burgoyne. It told him that Burgoyne was running out of supplies and that he had lost his line of communications back to Canada. Because of that message Burgoyne said that he planned to advance soon in order to join forces with Clinton. Clinton quickly gathered a 3,000-man force. With the first favorable tide (the Hudson River had high and low tides; sailing ships could only move up the river when the tides were right) Clinton moved up the Hudson.

Clinton's move surprised the Americans who were defending the Highlands. The rebel garrison at Verplanck fled. On October 5 Clinton received another message from Burgoyne. It said that Burgoyne's army was in a desperate situation. Burgoyne demanded that Clinton give him orders either to attack or to retreat. Such a demand was bad behavior on Burgoyne's part. Burgoyne was trying to shift the blame for his own failure to another general. Clinton understood what Burgoyne was trying to do, and he did not like it.

Burgoyne also wanted Clinton to capture Albany. Clinton knew that his force was too weak to do it. Still, Clinton tried to help Burgoyne as best he could. Clinton skillfully attacked the American forts near West Point that blocked the Hudson River. His men surprised the defenders by making a twelve-mile march through the woods in order to attack the forts from behind.

The strong American defenses on Bemis Heights forced Burgoyne to look for a way to move around the American position. This led to the second battle at Saratoga, the Battle of Bemis Heights.

Clinton's men captured the forts along with 67 cannons and many supplies. The Royal Navy broke through the barrier blocking the river and forced the complete destruction of the small rebel fleet that guarded the Hudson.

Clinton had done everything he could with his small army. On October 8 he sent a note to Burgoyne. It said that Clinton had cleared the Highlands and that now there was nothing between Clinton and Burgoyne except for Gates's army. But the Americans caught the messenger carrying Clinton's note and hanged him. So, Burgoyne did not know about Clinton's victory.

The Battle of Bemis Heights

After the Battle of Freeman's Farm Burgoyne's army dug trenches and built fortifications. Then the army waited. The army was not eating well. All the soldiers had was bread and dried pork. Some of their horses starved to death. Soldiers became sick, and many deserted. Losses from battle, sickness, and desertion reduced the army to about 5,000 regulars and 600 Canadian and loyalist allies.

While the British army grew weaker, Gates's army grew stronger. The militia who had fought at Bennington joined his army. News of the killing of Jane McCrea caused many other militia from New York and New England to come to Gates's army. About 11,000 soldiers, including 2,700 Continentals, manned the American defenses on Bemis Heights. They were happy about their recent success at Freeman's Farm. Everywhere in camp soldiers praised Arnold's courage and leadership at the battle.

Gates was jealous of Arnold's fame. Gates knew that Arnold badly wanted official praise from Congress and that he wanted promotion. To annoy Arnold, Gates sent Congress his report of the Battle of Freeman's Farm. Gates did not even mention that Arnold had done anything at the battle.

This insult deeply angered Arnold. He and Gates had a furious argument during which they shouted and cursed at one another. For ten days the ugly argument continued. Gates brought Benjamin Lincoln to camp to take charge of Arnold's men. Arnold threatened to leave

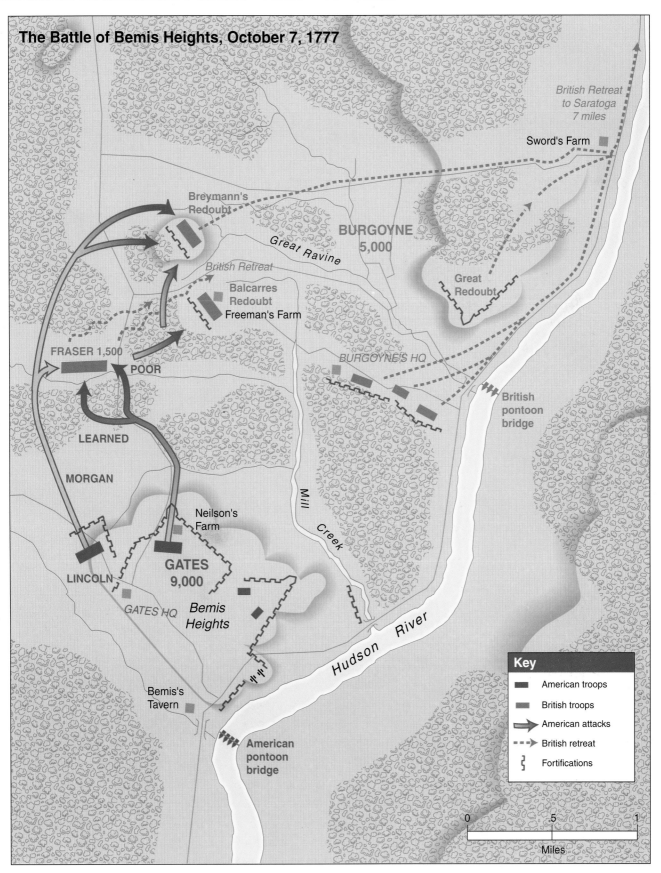

The Battle of Bemis Heights, October 7, 1777

British Retreat to Saratoga 7 miles

Sword's Farm

Breymann's Redoubt

BURGOYNE 5,000

Great Ravine

British Retreat

Balcarres Redoubt

Freeman's Farm

Great Redoubt

BURGOYNE'S HQ

FRASER 1,500

POOR

British pontoon bridge

LEARNED

MORGAN

Neilson's Farm

Mill Creek

GATES 9,000

LINCOLN

GATES HQ

Bemis Heights

Hudson River

Bemis's Tavern

American pontoon bridge

Key

■ American troops

■ British troops

→ American attacks

⇢ British retreat

ʃ Fortifications

0   5   1

Miles

American Major James Wilkinson alertly collected reports about Burgoyne's movements and informed Gates.

Enoch Poor's men bravely advanced into British artillery fire.

the army. But every American general except Gates and Lincoln signed a petition asking Arnold to stay. So, Arnold stayed in camp even though he had no troops to command.

As time passed, Burgoyne believed that the only way he could save his army was to push around or through Gates's position on Bemis Heights. But he still did not really know exactly where the American position was located. So, he planned a second big scouting mission. He hoped to find a way to attack the American left flank. Burgoyne sent 600 Canadian and Tory allies along with 1,500 regulars on the mission.

Around 10 A.M. on October 7, 1777, the British advanced from their trenches. They moved slowly for about two-thirds of a mile. They paused on a gentle rise where the officers tried to study the American position through their spyglasses. Meanwhile, hungry soldiers went into nearby fields to try to find food for themselves and their horses.

The Americans had watched the British advance. Major James Wilkinson collected the reports and informed Gates. Gates had learned from the first battle. This time he did not have to be convinced to fight. Daniel Morgan suggested that his riflemen attack. Gates agreed. Supposedly he said, "Order on Morgan to begin the game." The American plan was to stay in the woods and attack both British flanks.

The fight began when General Enoch Poor's 800 men attacked the British left. Poor's men coolly advanced through British artillery fire until they were close to the British grenadiers. Then they opened a deadly fire. The commander of the grenadiers, Major Acland, ordered his men to "Fix bayonets and charge the damned rebels." In the past the rebels had usually run when facing such an attack. This time several New Hampshire Continental regiments stood firm and fired a murderous volley that stopped the grenadiers. Among the British casualties was Acland, who fell with bullet wounds in both legs.

Meanwhile, Morgan attacked the British right flank. His Virginians easily drove off the Tories and Canadians. Then they opened fire against the flank and rear of the British position. The elite British light infantry tried to change position to charge Morgan. Dearborn's Continental Light Infantry arrived to catch the British before they could finish changing position. Dearborn's men fired and sent the British light infantry running.

Burgoyne ordered a retreat. But the officer carrying the order was wounded before he delivered the message. This left the Germans fighting against a much larger rebel force. General Ebenezer Learned was attacking the Germans in the front when up rode Arnold to lead the rebels.

Arnold rushed into the fight even though he had no authority to command any troops. In fact, Gates sent an officer to order Arnold to return to camp. Arnold ignored Gates's order. He led a series of furious attacks that drove the Germans back to a position called the Balcarres Redoubt. (A redoubt is a type of large earthwork. This one was named after a British officer.)

The British General Simon Fraser had been very active during the battle so far. He bravely rode his horse to wherever the fighting was the most dangerous. By his courage he rallied the British soldiers. Arnold saw Fraser and said to Daniel Morgan, "That man on the gray horse is a host [army] in himself and must be disposed of." One of Morgan's riflemen shot and killed Fraser. This discouraged the British, and they fell back to their original position.

The battle had lasted about 50 minutes so far. It would have ended at that point except for Arnold. In the words of a British military historian, "... with true military instinct [Arnold] seized the opportunity for a general attack upon the British entrenchments." Arnold was like a wild man. He rode from unit to unit to urge the rebels to charge. The rebels advanced against the Balcarres Redoubt only to be driven back by deadly British fire.

Since his men could not make progress there, Arnold rode across the field to see what could be done elsewhere. He passed between the lines, where he risked getting shot by soldiers on both sides. He followed a

Lady Acland's Journey

Lady Harriet Acland, married to the British officer Major John Acland, went with her husband to North America in 1776. Acland served in Burgoyne's campaign through the New York wilderness. Lady Acland traveled with the army and took care of her husband whenever he fell ill or got wounded.

Major Acland was shot in both legs and then captured by the Americans at the second Battle of Saratoga. Lady Acland heard of her husband's wound and got Burgoyne's permission to go join him. Lady Acland, two servants, and a British army chaplain bravely set out on the Hudson River in a small boat flying a white flag of truce. She had a note from General Burgoyne asking the American general Gates to treat her kindly. At first the guard did not want to let the boat land at the American camp, but eventually he received permission. General Gates provided Lady Acland with an escort to Albany. There she found her husband and cared for him among the Americans until he recovered enough to return to England.

good suggestion from Major Wilkinson and ordered an attack that captured a position between the Balcarres and Breymann redoubts (Breymann was the German officer who fought at Bennington). Their success let the Americans fire against the flank of the Breymann Redoubt. Then Arnold again rode to the other flank to lead a charge against the Breymann Redoubt.

Inside the redoubt was the brave and brutal Breymann. When Breymann's men began to run, Breymann attacked them with his sword "to keep them to their

The mortal wounding of the brave General Fraser discouraged the British troops.

Arnold's attacks drove the British back to Balcarres Redoubt, marked on the battlefield by these two artillery pieces.

work." One of Breymann's own men shot and killed him. The capture of the Breymann Redoubt forced the British to retreat. Darkness saved the British army from total defeat.

The Battle of Bemis Heights, or the Second Battle of Saratoga, cost the Americans only about 150 casualties. Late in the fighting Arnold received a wound to the same leg that had been hit during the Quebec Campaign. The British lost about 600 men and eight to ten cannons.

After his defeat Burgoyne had to retreat from the area. First, his men moved back to a large fortification by the river called the Great Redoubt. Then, during the night of October 8 Burgoyne skillfully led his army away from the battlefield. Burgoyne ordered an act of revenge by having his men burn the mansion belonging to Philip Schuyler.

Gates pursued until he had Burgoyne surrounded on three sides. Only a gap leading north remained. Burgoyne hoped to withdraw through that gap. He had just issued orders to try to escape when he learned that John Stark had moved a force to block his route. Burgoyne was trapped by an American force that numbered nearly 20,000 men. Burgoyne had no choice but to surrender.

The Significance of Saratoga

About 5,000 British, German, Canadian, and Tory soldiers surrendered at Saratoga. According to an agreement between Burgoyne and Gates, the British

When the British prisoners marched past the generals, Burgoyne handed Gates his sword as a symbol of his surrender. Gates handed the sword back to Burgoyne to honor both Burgoyne and his men.

army was supposed to give up its weapons, march to Boston, and then sail back to England. They had to promise not to fight in America again.

When Congress learned about the agreement, they believed that it was a bad deal. Congressmen thought that the British prisoners would simply be used somewhere else and so free other British soldiers to come to America. So, Congress broke the agreement and forced the prisoners to stay in America.

The defeat of Burgoyne at Saratoga was the turning point in the Revolutionary War because it led to an alliance between the United States and France. Without the French alliance the revolution would have failed.

The victory also came at a time when American morale was low because the British had defeated Washington's army and captured the capital at Philadelphia (see Volume 6). The victory encouraged the rebels throughout the thirteen colonies to keep fighting.

A long struggle lay ahead. There would be many times

when it seemed that the rebel cause would collapse. Only later would people really have a chance to think about what had taken place at Saratoga. Once the war was over and people looked back, the importance of Saratoga became clear. It had been the decisive battle of the Revolutionary War, a battle that changed world history.

The British prisoners marched to Boston, where they expected to board ships to return to England. Congress broke the agreement and kept the prisoners in America.

Chronology

December 26, 1776: George Washington and his army win the Battle of Trenton, New Jersey.

January 3, 1777: Washington and his army surprise and defeat the British at the Battle of Princeton, New Jersey.

June 18, 1777: Burgoyne and his army begin the planned invasion of New York state.

July 6, 1777: The rebels retreat from Fort Ticonderoga without a fight.

August 1777: The rebels learn that Indians fighting on the British side have killed a young woman, Jane McRea. The news outrages the Americans, causing hundreds to join the rebel militia.

August 2–23, 1777: British Lieutenant Colonel Barry St. Leger and a force of British, loyalist, Canadian, and Indian troops lay siege to American troops at Fort Stanwix.

August 6, 1777: American militia engage a force of Mohawk Indians fighting for the British at the Battle of Oriskany in New York state.

August 16, 1777: American militia beat professional German soldiers fighting for the British at Bennington, Vermont.

August 23, 1777: Major General Benedict Arnold and a force of 950 men arrive to relieve the New York Continentals at Fort Stanwix.

September 19, 1777: The Battle of Freeman's Farm, Saratoga, New York. The British hold their ground and claim victory, but actually lose more men than the Americans.

October 3, 1777: Sir Henry Clinton departs on a campaign through the Hudson Highlands to distract the Americans from Burgoyne's stranded army to the north.

October 7, 1777: The Battle of Bemis Heights, or the second Battle of Saratoga, ends in defeat for the British. Burgoyne is forced to surrender about 5,000 men.

December 17, 1777: Learning of the American victory at Saratoga, France recognizes American independence.

Glossary

ALLIANCE: agreement between two nations to fight on the same side in a war

ARTILLERY: a group of cannons and other large guns used to help an army by firing at enemy troops

BAYONET: a sword attached to the muzzle of a musket or rifle

BRIGADE: an army unit made up of four or more regiments. Three or more brigades make up a division.

CAMPAIGN: a series of military actions that are connected because they have the same goal

CASUALTIES: people wounded, killed, or missing after a battle

CAVALRY: a group of soldiers who move and fight on horseback

COLUMN: a narrow, deep formation in which soldiers stand in many ranks behind the front rank. The most common column is a road column, in which the front rank is as wide as the road, and the rest of the soldiers march behind the front rank.

CONTINENTALS: soldiers serving in the regular American army

DEFENSES: a line of fieldworks and forts around an area that an army is defending

DESERTER: a soldier or sailor who leaves the army or navy without permission

ENLISTMENT: signing up to join an army or navy; a term of enlistment is the agreed time that one will stay in the military

FLANK: one side of an army on a battlefield

GARRISON: the group of soldiers stationed at a fort or military post

GRENADIER: specially chosen men who make up an elite group of infantry soldiers

HESSIANS: hired German soldiers who fought for the British. The Americans called all German mercenaries "Hessians."

INDIANS: the name given to all Native Americans at the time Europeans settled the New World. The name was chosen because the first European explorers thought the New World was part of India.

INFANTRY: foot soldiers, or soldiers who march and fight on foot

LIGHT INFANTRY: an elite group of foot soldiers selected for their ability to move and think quickly

MILITIA: a group of citizens not normally part of the army who organize for the purpose of defending their homeland in an emergency; also used as a plural to describe several such groups

RAISE: to build up a military force by getting new soldiers to enlist or by gathering soldiers from other units

REDOUBT: a temporary stronghold or fortification, often built in front of an army's main position

REGIMENT: an army unit made up of ten companies. A regiment at full strength had about 450 soldiers.

REGULARS: professional soldiers who belong to the army full time

REINFORCEMENTS: additional soldiers sent to help an army either before or during a battle

ROUT: disorderly retreat or panicked flight from the battlefield

SIEGE: a campaign to capture a place by surrounding it, cutting it off from supplies, and attacking it cautiously under the cover of trenches and earthworks

STRATEGY: the overall plan for a battle or campaign

SUPPLY LINE: the route used to bring supplies from the base to an army in the field

TORY: an American colonist who sided with England during the American Revolution; also called loyalist

WINTER QUARTERS: where armies camped during the winter

Further Resources

Books:

Adams, Russell B., Jr., ed. *The Revolutionaries*. Alexandria, VA: Time-Life Books, 1996.

Bliven, Bruce, Jr. *The American Revolution*. New York: Random House, 1986.

Dolan, Edward F. *The American Revolution: How We Fought the War of Independence*. Brookfield, CT: Millbrook Press, 1995.

King, David. *Benedict Arnold and the American Revolution*. Woodbridge, CT: Blackbirch, 1998.

King, David. *Saratoga*. New York: 21st Century Books, 1998.

Martin, J. P. *Private Yankee Doodle*. Fort Washington, PA: Eastern Acorn Press, 1998. The entire diary of Joseph Plumb Martin, who enlisted in the Continental Army when he was 15.

Wilbur, C. Keith. *The Revolutionary Soldier, 1775-1783*. Old Saybrook, CT: Globe Pequot Press, 1993.

Websites:

http://library.thinkquest.org/10966/
The Revolutionary War—A Journey Towards Freedom

ushistory.org/march/index.html
Virtual Marching Tour of the American Revolution

http://www.pbs.org/ktca/liberty/game/index.html
The Road to Revolution—A Revolutionary Game

http://www.pbs.org/ktca/liberty/chronicle/index.html
Chronicle of the Revolution
Read virtual newspapers of the Revolutionary era

http://www.fort-ticonderoga.org
Official website of Fort Ticonderoga Museum

http://www.nps.gov/sara/
Official website of Saratoga National Historical Park

Places to Visit:

Bennington Museum, Bennington, Vermont

Fort Ticonderoga Museum, Ticonderoga, New York

Saratoga National Historical Park, Stillwater, New York

About the Authors

James R. Arnold has written more than 20 books on military history topics and contributed to many others. Roberta Wiener has coauthored several books with Mr. Arnold and edited numerous educational books, including a children's encyclopedia. They live and farm in Virginia.

Set Index

Bold numbers refer to volumes; *italics* refer to illustrations

Acknowledgments

Architect of the Capitol: Title page, 64–65
Author's collection: 8B, 30, 50, 57, 60B, 63
Ballou's Pictorial: 42–43
Bennington Museum, Bennington, Vermont: 36–37, 38–39
Eldridge S. Brooks, *The Century Book of the American Revolution*, 1897: 31
Anne S. K. Brown Military Collection, John Hay Library, Brown University, Providence, Rhode Island: 25, 34–35, 47
Charles C. *Coffin Boys of '76*, 1876: 35, 54
Fort Ticonderoga Museum: 32T, 66–67
Independence National Historical Park: 32B, 41, 51, 60T
Library of Congress:, 9, 16, 19, 28, 29, 42T, 61
Military Archive & Research Services, England: 18
National Archives: 7, 8T, 20, 21T, 22, 26, 27, 33, 40, 48, 52, 56
National Archives of Canada: 62–63
U.S. Naval Historical Center, Washington, D.C.: 12–13, 45
U.S. Government Printing Office: Front cover, 6, 10, 11, 17, 53
Henry C. Watson, *Campfires of the Revolution*, 1858: 55
Bernard Wiener: 21B
Robert W. Wilson, Woodruff, SC: 24

Maps by Jerry Malone